T0149642

PRAYING FOR OUR
PRECIOUS CHILDREN

FULFILLING OUR PURPOSE BY
TURNING OUR PAINS TO PRAYERS

SHARMELA GOKOOL

PRAYING FOR OUR PRECIOUS CHILDREN
FULFILLING OUR PURPOSE BY TURNING OUR PAINS TO PRAYERS

iUniverse books may be ordered through booksellers or by contacting:

iUniverse
1663 Liberty Drive
Bloomington, IN 47403
www.iuniverse.com
1-800-Authors (1-800-288-4677)

Scripture quotations marked KJV are from the Holy Bible, King James Version (Authorized Version). First published in 1611. Quoted from the KJV Classic Reference Bible, Copyright © 1983 by The Zondervan Corporation.

ISBN: 978-1-5320-7914-6 (sc)
ISBN: 978-1-5320-7915-3 (e)

Library of Congress Control Number: 2019910606

Print information available on the last page.

iUniverse rev. date: 07/25/2019

I will therefore that men pray everywhere, lifting up holy hands
without wrath and doubting
1ˢᵗ Timothy 2:8

This book

"Praying for Our Precious Children"

Is presented to:

_____

With Love from:

_____

On:

_____

CONTENTS

INTRODUCTION

This series of Praying for Our Precious Children is a vision I had received from God. It was on February 18ᵗʰ 2017 the day my 3ʳᵈ born son Adrion would have turned two (2) years old.

I woke up about 4:00am to pray for Adrion. Not only because it was his birthday I woke up that time, it's because I am always in prayer that time of the morning. And while I was praying for my son I saw a "darkness" over him.

In the vision he was sitting in front of me but the very atmosphere around my son was like dark smoke and I saw a hand around my son neck as if he is being choked to remain silent.

Imagine we can be so amazed even in the midst of prayer the kind of things the Lord shows and reveals to us. But I thanked God that He had revealed it to me and immediately from that moment on my prayer life had changed.

My prayers had made a big shift to a higher level. The Lord led me to fast and pray to destroy the plans the devil had against my son Adrion to destroy his voice and his purpose which He had revealed to me.

During my pray and fast the Lord led me to pray for all the children on earth. And the more I would pray is the more the Lord would reveal to me what to pray for. I heard the cries of mothers and fathers in the spirit for their children who have suffered untimely deaths and accidents.

In visions I saw children and youths bounded by all kinds of dark forces and chains of the enemy. I became more and more passionate of this assignment the Lord had trusted me with.

I started posting "prayers" for children on my "Facebook" page so I know when others read them, it would be as if they were really touching in agreement to pray for all our children as well.

I become more heartened when parents started to message me on "Facebook messenger" asking me to pray for their kids and some even asked for "prayers" that they can pray and speak over their children lives every day.

Those that requested pray for their kids opened my heart because we all need a direction on how to pray for them when situations arise. Just as a child needs training to grow, we also need the encouragement and support from each other, and to more importantly to prayer for one another.

"Two are better than one; because they have a good reward for their labour.
For if they fall, the one will lift up his fellow: but woe to him that is alone when he falleth; for he hath not another to help him up".
Ecclesiastes 4:9-10

And I wanted to do more than just post on Facebook social media, I wanted the rest of the world to know what to pray for as well. I thirsted for more of God's glory to be revealed in and through me which is the beauty of God's goodness, He will give us more than we ask.

As time passed by I was eager for others to know the things God had revealed for us to pray for our children that will protect them and will open the flood gates of Heaven over their lives.

"For where two or three are gathered together in
my name, there am I in the midst of them."
Mathew 18:20

It was on June 1st 2019 I was led by the Spirit of the Lord to compose a "Prayer Book" for all parents, teachers and leaders to pray for our children and set them free from the hands of the wicked and evil one.

This book is a proof that I am entirely assured that many nations are praying for our precious children now.

So I guarantee you beloved prayer warrior, you and your children shall be blessed and strengthen from glory to glory because you have invested your time to pray for all children.

God was truly determined for this book to be published for His children to be set free and to walk in their purpose. And I thank God for you, for choosing you in a time like this to advance your prayer to another level and stand as a watchman for all our precious children.

God's Blessings to you Precious Prayer Warrior and congratulations on your new level in God.

"Ye also by helping together by prayer for us that for
the gifts bestowed upon us by he means of many persons
thanks may be given by many on our behalf"
2 Corinthians 1:11

ACKNOWLEDGEMENTS

Render therefore to all their dues: tribute to whom tribute is due; custom to whom custom; fear to whom fear; honour to whom honour.
Romans 13:7

Firstly and fore mostly I would like to say:
*"**THANK YOU LORD**" for your Divine Blessings upon my life. Without you Lord, this book would have not been possible.*

Thank you, Jesus, for this Vision to stand in the gap for Every Child in this Universe. Thank you, Lord, for your merciful love towards me and for blessing me with four (4) Precious Children of my own, Satesh, Ranjeev, Adrion and Emily. They are reasons I can share with others what you have revealed to me how and why we must pray for our precious children.

Now unto the King eternal, immortal, invisible, the only wise God, be honour and glory forever and ever
1 Timothy 1:17

*I thank God also for the "**Family**" of **Chosen Deliverance Centre**, Trinidad. It is there I got saved, I was welcomed as a sinner on June 19th 2019 and I gave my life to Christ that day and since I have got saved I have never turned back to my same old ways.*
I thank God that He has used this Ministry to draw me into the Body of Christ because I was welcomed with love as if God himself had

welcomed me home. Now I have become a part of this family in Christ to fulfil one of my purpose for God which was to write this book.

I pray the Lord continue to elevate your Ministry, the Leaders and the children of Chosen Deliverance Centre with more visions and provisions for the advancement of His Kingdom.

Let the elders that rule well be counted worthy of double honour, especially they who labour in the word and doctrine.
1 Timothy 5:17

With deep gratitude thank you to my loving, humble and kind husband **Rondon Noor** for all your support to start this new journey. I pray the Lord continue to bless your hard-working hands and keep shining His Divine Light in and through you for His Divine Honour and Glory. I love you.

And he shall be like a tree planted by the rivers of water, that bringeth forth his fruit in his season; his leaf also shall not wither, and whatsoever he doeth shall prosper
Psalms 1:3

Special thanks to a **Daughter of Zion Sister Myrna Joseph** for encouraging me to open the "Praying for Our Precious Children Page" on Facebook that was led to this book which has touched families in many nations. Sister Myrna Joseph may the Lord continue to use you in a mighty way to lift up women of many nations.

And God is able to make all grace abound to you; that ye; always having all sufficiency in all things; may abound to every good work
2nd Corinthians 9:8

To my dear **Sister Maureen Cudjoe**, you are a blessing to me. No matter what, time or day you would consistently encourage me to walk faithfully and serve the Lord. Thank you for investing in this book with *your dedications and prayer. You shall not go unrewarded Precious Woman of God.*

He will love you, bless you, and multiply you. He will also bless the fruit of your womb and the fruit of your ground, your grain and your wine and your oil, the increase of your herds and the young of your flock, in the land that he swore to your fathers to give you Deuteronomy 7:13

TESTIMONIES

I am Hazel-Ann, of Trinidad, West Indies and am honoured to share my Testimony about who I know Sharmela Gokool to be.

"Sharmela to me has been a family oriented Blessed and Highly favoured Prayer Warrior who truly loves the Lord". I must confess after she created the page:
"Praying for Our Precious Children", I saw her in a different light.

She proved herself to be a passionate, dedicated daughter of our most high God and Our Lord and Saviour Jesus Christ; a Mighty Woman Of God who knows how to war, how to bombard the Heavens and how to P.U.S.H. in Prayer.
She knows without a doubt we are in a warzone, it's a continuous battle in which if the enemy can't have us he will definitely wipe out what's most valuable to us; i.e.; our 'Precious Children'; yes he is after the fruit of our wombs; the seed of the loins of our men (husband's, brothers etc.).
She knows if we cease to pray we cease to fight and giving up is not an option. She knows we we're created to Worship, and how to get Heaven's attention. I can boldly say: in the realm of the Spirit she's one of the devil's worst nightmare!
Sharmela puts God first and foremost in every walk of life as a result she has been a blessing to many including myself. She is and will continue to be an inspiration and a motivator to the many persons that will cross her pathway. I dedicate the following scripture to this book

For who hath despised the day of small things? For they shall rejoice,
and shall see the plummet in the hand of Zerubbabel with those seven;
they are the eyes of the Lord, which run through the whole earth
Zechariah 4:10

And to the Author Beloved Sharmela

The Lord shall open unto me His good treasure, the
heaven "to give the rain unto thy land in his season, and
to bless all they work of thine hand; and thou shalt lend
unto many nations, and thou shall not borrow."
Deuteronomy 28:12

My name is Vera Sampson of Trinidad, West Indies and this is my testimony of the Author of this book.

I was introduced to Sister Sharmela Gokool since the beginning of this year 2019 through her sister Shivanie Ali- Gokool and since then Sharmela has been encouraging me daily with prayers and words of encouragement for me to see my son go through chemo in such a tender age.

Sharmela helped me to be still and stand despite how difficult it was and to trust God even more than ever and it was not long after we witness a miracle when my son's tumour in his arm disappeared.

She has a passion to help others so much that she also helped me to find a job, which proves of her kindness and patience towards others. Today I am thankful that the Lord is using her in His Kingdom and for bringing her into my life.

I dedicate these few words to Sister Sharmela

You are an encourager when I was down and you helped me to regain strength to see my son through his chemo. I thank God for using you, for your prayers and bringing you in my life. You have showed me when we face problems we have to learn to look at How Big Our God is. May God bless you and I pray you continue to be a strength to others to keep a positive journey to trust God in all things. God Bless You.

A
Guide
To the
Prayer Warrior
How to fulfil your purpose by
turning your pains into prayers

Confess *your* faults one to another, and pray one
for another, that ye may be healed. The effectual
fervent prayer of a righteous man availeth much.
James 5:16

WHAT IS PRAYER?

Prayer is the only link between us and God. We cannot see God, but we believe there is a God and we believe His Son Jesus Christ is our Lord and Saviour.

God hears us when we pray. He is always eager to answer our prayers when we call on Him.

All throughout the bible we can grasp that prayer is required for us to lead, follow, guide, teach, preach, worship and praise God for the things He has already done for us and thank Him for the things He is about to do.

Prayer is what we must do to accomplish anything we desire.

Prayer is the only solution we have when we find ourselves in problems and to have no problems in our life we must pray.

Our prayer is a Divine Conversation with God. If we are not praying we have absolutely no communication with God.

Without prayer we are nothing. We may be alive but really without prayer we are spiritually dead.

Prayer activates our faith for the unseen things and it gives us hope for the future.

Prayer changes things and the way we see and feel about any situation. It moves us from a negative mood to a positive attitude.

Prayer unlocks hidden gifts that we have been birthed with and planted within us.

Prayer reveals the mystery, signs and wonders of God that no man has seen or heard of before.

Pray is putting everything in God's control, no matter what the outcome may be; it positions us to a place of understanding and growth.

Prayer changes the way we see situations no matter how bad it may seem, we will not be confused about it but will see the goodness of God in it.

Prayer is an act of worship of the presence of God because God is omnipresent. He is here, there and everywhere. So no matter where we are, what we are doing God hears our prayers.

Prayer reveals the characteristics of who God is in our lives.

Prayer turns our normal and ordinary life into a spiritual and passionate life to please God and obey His Word.

"Be careful for nothing; but in everything by prayer and supplication with thanks giving let your request be made known unto God, and the peace of God which passeth all understanding shall keep your hearts and minds through Christ Jesus"
Philippians 4: 6-7

"If my people who are called by my name, shall humble themselves, and pray and seek my face, and turn from their wicked ways; then I will hear from heaven, and will forgive their sin and will heal their land"
2nd Chronicles 7:14

HOW WE MUST PRAY?

Hear, ye children, the instruction of a Father, and attend to know
understanding. For I give you good doctrine, forsake ye not my law
Proverbs 4:1

The Lord has revealed to us in His Word there are many ways how
we must pray and why we must pray.

We must prepare ourselves to go before God, by not taking for granted
who He is but by acknowledging Him that He is the Highest and
Greatest King of Kings and the Lord of Lord's over all.

Always remember obeying Instructions from God is the best way we
can be sure of receiving all that we have asked for in prayer according
to His will.

Ye are all the children of light, and the children of the
day: we are not of the night, nor of darkness.

✓ *Therefore let us not sleep, as do others; but let us watch and be*
sober.
For they that sleep, sleep in the night; and they
that be drunken are drunken in the night.
✓ *But let us, who are of the day, be sober,*
✓ *putting on the breastplate of faith and love;*
✓ *and for an helmet, the hope of salvation.*
For God hath not appointed us to wrath,
✓ *but to obtain salvation by our Lord Jesus Christ,*

Who died for us, that, whether we wake or sleep,
✓ *we should live together with him.*
✓ *Wherefore comfort yourselves together,*
✓ *and edify one another, even as also ye do.*
And we beseech you, brethren,
✓ *to know them which labour among you, and are over you in the Lord, and admonish you;*
✓ *And to esteem them very highly in love for their work's sake.*
✓ *And be at peace among yourselves.*

Now we exhort you, brethren,
✓ *warn them that are unruly,*
✓ *comfort the feebleminded,*
✓ *support the weak,*
✓ *be patient toward all men.*
✓ *See that none render evil for evil unto any man; but ever follow that which is good, both among yourselves, and to all men.*
✓ *Rejoice evermore.*
✓ *Pray without ceasing.*
✓ *In every thing give thanks: for this is the will of God in Christ Jesus concerning you.*
✓ *Quench not the Spirit.*
✓ *Despise not prophesyings.*
✓ *Prove all things; hold fast that which is good.*
✓ *Abstain from all appearance of evil.*

And the very God of peace sanctify you wholly; and I pray God your whole spirit and soul and body be preserved blameless unto the coming of our Lord Jesus Christ.

Faithful is he that calleth you, who also will do it.
✓ *Brethren, pray for us.*
✓ *Greet all the brethren with an holy kiss.*

✓ *I charge you by the Lord that this epistle be read unto all the holy brethren.*

The grace of our Lord Jesus Christ be with you. Amen.

1ˢᵗ Thessalonians 5:5-28

And the bible also declares in

Ephesians 6:11-24

✓ *Put on the whole armour of God,*
That ye may be able to stand against the wiles of the devil.
For we wrestle not against flesh and blood, but against
principalities, against powers, against the rulers of the darkness
of this world, against spiritual wickedness in high places.
✓ *Wherefore take unto you the whole armour of God that ye may*
be able to withstand in the evil day, and having done all, to
stand.
✓ *Stand therefore, having your loins girt about with truth, and*
✓ *having on the breastplate of righteousness;*

✓ *And your feet shod with the preparation of the gospel of peace;*
✓ *Above all, taking the shield of faith, wherewith ye shall be able*
to quench all the fiery darts of the wicked.
✓ *And take the helmet of SALVATION, and*
✓ *the SWORD OF THE SPIRIT, which is the WORD*
OF GOD:
✓ *PRAYING always with all prayer and supplication in the*
Spirit, and
✓ *WATCHING thereunto with all perseverance and supplication*
for all saints;

STEP 1: GLORIFY GOD

Our relationship with God determines who we see and know God as. He is the Divine Creator of all things. He is all Holy all Powerful, all Righteous, all Merciful, all Faithful, all Loving and He deserve all our Glory, all our Worship and all our Praises. So when we go before God by honouring Him we are giving reverence to His Presence as the measure of His Love and Mercy towards us which is a heartfelt, gracious and humble gratitude.

Thou art worthy, O Lord, to receive glory and honour
and power: for thou hast created all things, and
for thy pleasure they are and were created
Revelation 4:11

STEP 2: REPENTING OF OUR SINS

Repent and ask God for the forgiveness of all sins we may have committed known, and unknown. Repentance frees us from the bondage of sin and it arrests us in the Holy Spirit realm to prayer and activate in the Spirit of God.

This is called "True Repentance" where we are not only repenting but convicted to change and never remain the same again.

If we confess our sins, he is faithful and just to forgive us
our sins, and to cleanse us from all unrighteousness
1ˢᵗ John 1:9

STEP 3: WORSHIP THE LORD

Sing High Praises unto God. Glorify His Name, Worship Him in Spirit and In Truth.

When we worship before we pray, giving reverence to the Holy Presence of God, the very atmosphere changes. Our minds and hearts changes into a sacred platform.

I will praise thee, O Lord my God, with all my heart:
and I will glorify thy name for evermore
Psalm 86:12

O worship the Lord in the beauty of holiness:
fear before him, all the earth
Psalm 96:9-11

STEP 4: ASK & YOU SHALL RECEIVE

Make your request known to God and believe that what you ask for, you shall receive it. What you are seeking for, you will surely find it and what you are knocking on doors for God to open He will surely open it to you.

God sees us as His "PRAYER" and we must see Him as Our "PROVIDER".

> *Whatever you ask in my name, that will I do, so*
> *that the Father may be glorified in the Son*
> *John 14:13*

In the book of Mathew Chapter 7 verse 8 the Lord reassures us that if we:

✓ *Ask, and it shall be given you;*
✓ *seek, and ye shall find;*
✓ *knock, and it shall be opened unto you:*
✓ *For every one that asketh receiveth; and*
✓ *he that seeketh findeth, and to*
✓ *him that knocketh it shall be opened"*

STEP. 5: ACTIVATING OUR FAITH

Give thanks in advance for your Victory in Faith that your prayers has been answered. Faith is what moves the hand of God. Faith gives us rest of mind. Our "Faith" is activated by "believing we have received what we have asked for" and by giving "Thanks in advance".

In everything give thanks; for this is the will of
God in Christ Jesus concerning you
1ˢᵗ Thessalonians 5:18

Therefore I say unto you, whatsoever things you desire, when ye pray, believe that ye receive them, and ye shall have them
Mark 11:24

WHY IT IS IMPORTANT TO PRAY FOR OUR PRECIOUS CHILDREN.

No matter what age our children are we have the right to constantly lift them up to our Heavenly Father. When our children hear and see us praying for them and others; they will do the same.

We must teach our children that "to pray" is the only solution for any situation. When our children see us in prayer, we will be teaching them the significance and importance of Prayer.

They will begin to manifest in that Divine and Glorious impact in Building and Making a Relationship with God even from a tender age.

They will have the joy to talk to God and go to God freely and they will grow a love for God that will cause them to do the Perfect Will of God and obey His Word.

When our children hear us pray for them they will also do the same and pray for themselves in times of trouble and they will eventually start praying for us their parents and for other children as well.

So, I encourage you, never stop praying for your children, my children and all children because I assure you, prayer warrior you are fulfilling the Will of God.

I declare you shall see great and mighty things from God done through you when you allow God to use your vessel to pray for others especially our young generation that is coming up.

*And He (Jesus) spake a parable unto them to this end,
that men ought always to pray, and not to faint
Luke 18:1*

*I love you and God loves you because we are all His own precious
children.*

From your Beloved Sister in Christ

LET US PRAYER
For Our
PRECIOUS CHILDREN

I exhort therefore, that, first of all,
supplications, prayers, intercessions, and
giving thanks, be made of all men
1 Timothy 2:1

1
PRAYER AGAINST REBELLIOUSNESS

Heavenly Father Lord we come boldly before your throne and we bring our precious children before you Lord. Father, we ask that by your mighty power dismantle every spirit of rebelliousness that our children are operating in. Lord let our children be loosed from this stronghold of the enemy.

Father we declare and decree by your word that our children are a product of you. They have the image, the ways and the likeness of you according to your Divine Will.

Lord let nothing but the Holy Spirit of the true and living God reside in our children's lives to guide them in their going out and coming in.

Father may our children be transformed now in Jesus Name to your perfect will and they shall be pleasing unto you to fulfil your purpose here on earth that you have assigned to them that will cause them to make a difference for the generation to come after them for your Glory in Jesus Name.

Father Every generational curse of rebelliousness from our mother's ancestry, our father's ancestry, our mother in law's ancestry and our father in law's ancestry be broken now from four (4) generations back from our children's lives in Jesus Name.

Lord, we plead the undefeated blood of Jesus Christ over our children's lives to destroy every evil work of the enemy that our children are deceived to do in Jesus Name.

Spirit of rebellion by the Power and Authority in Christ Jesus we command you to leave our children's lives and never return in the Name of Jesus Christ of Nazareth.

Father, we declare and decree our children are completely and perfectly delivered from this spirit of rebellion in Jesus Name.

Our children shall live free from this bondage for eternity and every root of rebelliousness in their lives and the root cause of it shall be consumed to ashes now with the consuming fire of God in Jesus Name. Rebelliousness shall never rise again in their lives in the Mighty and Powerful Name of Jesus Christ of Nazareth.

Father, we thank you Lord that the kingdom of darkness has no rule or residence in our children's lives in Jesus Mighty Name. Our children are delivered into your Marvellous Light to live and only glorify you in Jesus Name.

We declare & decree from this day forth our children shall walk in your perfect will and shall dwell in your Heavenly Divine Spiritual Blessings, Wisdom and Knowledge that is in Christ Jesus for eternity in Jesus Mighty and Precious Name
AMEN

Children, obey your parents in the Lord, for this is right. "Honour thy father and mother; (which is the first commandment with promise). That it may be well with thee, and thou mayest live long on the earth Ephesians 6:1-3

And, ye fathers, provoke not your children to wrath: but bring them up in the nurture and admonition of the Lord Ephesians 6:4

For rebellion is as the sin of witchcraft, and stubbornness is as iniquity and idolatry. Because thou hast rejected the word of Lord, he hath also rejected thee from being king 1st Samuel 15:23

2
PRAYER FOR SUCCESS

Heavenly Father we thank you Lord for our children. We give you all Glory all honour and all the praise that belongs to you alone for just who you are, for all that you have done and for all that you are about to do in Jesus Name.

Lord, we thank you for keeping our children aligned to your will. Father, we ask that you increased in our children wisdom. Let the power of your promise manifest in our children's lives in Jesus Name. We declare and decree by the Power and Authority of Christ Jesus that our children shall be successful in every area of their life.

Every exam sheet, term paper, projects, assignments and academic achievements they set their hearts to do or given to do this season, we declare and decree that they shall pass with High-Speed Victory through the Power and Guidance of your Holy Spirit.

Lord let your angels guide them to seek you for Wisdom in everything they set their hearts to do as they grow older. The wisdom that will far exceed what we may think or see. We declare and decree our children shall manifest in your Divine Wisdom, Knowledge and Understanding in Jesus Name.

Whatever our children set their hearts to do physically, financially, academically, mentally, literally and spiritually it shall come to pass according to your will in Jesus Name.

Lord we declare and decree by your promised word that your plans to prosper our children, to keep them from evil and to give them a hope and a future shall be planted and birthed in our children's minds and hearts in Jesus Name.

Our children shall hear your voice and obey it. They shall run through troops and leap over walls because their eyes shall be revealed of the next path you have set before them. Father, we place our children into your mighty hands and we ask that you keep and bless them, cause your face to shine on them and uphold them with your right hand in Jesus Name.

We thank you, Lord that our children are overcomers of the things of this world and former things of the past in Jesus Name.

We declare and decree our children shall continuously walk into New Levels of Success all the days of their lives that will cause them to enter new doors of greater achievements. Father they shall be a blessing to many revealing your Glory through them in Jesus Name.

AMEN

If any of you lack wisdom, let him ask of God, that giveth to all men liberally, and upbraideth not; and it shall be given him
James 1:5

Call unto me, and I will answer thee, and shew thee great and mighty things Which thou knowest not
Jeremiah 33:3

Get wisdom, get understanding: forget it not; neither decline from the words of my mouth
Proverbs 4:5

Study to shew thyself approved unto God, a workman that needeth not to be ashamed, rightly dividing the word of truth
2nd Timothy 2:15

3
PRAYER FOR OUR NEW BORN BABIES

Heavenly Father we adore you, Lord. We give you praise and thanks for your precious gift of this child. We glorify your name which is the highest for the marvellous work you have placed into our hands.

Lord our child shall have life and life abundantly in good health as a new creation birthed and raised in God. Father, we bless you for blessing us with this beautiful gem from Heaven.

Lord, we ask that whatever your plans are for our child it shall surely come to pass in Jesus Name.

Lord pour unto us your Divine Wisdom to grow him/her up in the way that he/she should go and when he/she are old enough he/she will not depart from it in Jesus Name.

Lord, we ask that you use our child from this tender age for your honour and glory. Father activate our spirit of discernment to know your thoughts that shall guide us the chosen parents to raise our child as a vessel you shall use on this earth to glorify your Holy & Precious Name.

Father, we declare that every person under the spirit of destruction against our precious little angel will not come near our child in Jesus Name.

Lord, we ask that you place your mighty hand as a hedge of protection over our child that no one will be able to hurt your little one in anyway and no weapon formed or fashioned against our child shall prosper.

Father our child shall never suffer any untimely death, untimely injury, untimely accident and untimely sickness in Jesus Name.

We declare and decree that our child shall walk, talk, think and operate in the image and likeness as your son Jesus all the days of his/her life that you can surely say this is "My child in whom I am well pleased".

Father by your awesome and wonderful powers we declare our child is a New Creation in Christ Jesus and shall never depart from it in Jesus Name.

We declare and decree our child shall live to reveal too many that Jesus Christ is Lord and Saviour all the days of his/her life from everlasting to everlasting in Jesus Name.

AMEN

> *Lo, children are an heritage of the Lord: and the fruit of the womb is his reward. As arrows are in the hand of a mighty man, so are the children of the youth*
> *Psalm 127:3-4*

> *For this child I prayed; and the Lord has granted me my petition which I asked of him: Therefore I have lent him to the Lord. As long as he liveth, he shall be lent to the Lord." And he worshiped the Lord there*
> *1st Samuel 1:27-28*

4
PRAYER FOR HEALING

Heavenly Father we glorify your Holy Name. Lord we just say thank you wonderful counsellor for just who you are.

Lord, we lift our children before you and we ask that you heal our children from this sickness.

Lord by your word we declare sickness is not of you it is of the devil and we command the devil to let go of our children's lives, bodies and soul now in Jesus Name.

We declare in Jesus Name every spirit of infirmity is broken off from our children's lives now in Jesus Name.

We declare and decree every spirit of affliction is broken off now from our children's lives in Jesus Name.

Jehovah Rapha mighty healer God we ask that you pluck out from the root all forms of sickness, virus and disease from our children's lives and heal them in Jesus Name.

We declare and decree our children are healed and delivered from all manner of sickness, disease and afflictions aware and unaware in Jesus Name.

By the mighty finger of God, every form of sickness known and unknown is plucked out from the root and the root cause of it from our children's lives now in Jesus Name.

We thank you Lord God Jehovah Rapha Mighty Healer our children are healed and delivered from every form of sickness in Jesus Name.

We thank you Lord God Jehovah Rapha Mighty Healer our children are free of all form and fashion of sickness from the crown of their heads to the very sole of their feet in the Mighty and Powerful Name of Jesus Christ of Nazareth.

Lord we ask for your complete healing and restoration unto our children that they be healed in every area of their life emotionally, physically, socially, mentally, academically and spiritually in Jesus Name.

Lord, we declare and decree that every bone, every muscle, every organ and every tissue cell in their bodies shall operate satisfactorily and perform well to do what you have created and designed it to do from the day of Adam in the Name of Jesus.

Father our children are overcomers of all sickness now through the blood of the lamb and the words of their testimony in Jesus Name.

Father, we declare your glorious marvellous hands over our children's lives that every entrance the devil used to bring sickness in their lives is shut and covered with the blood of Jesus.

We declare and decree the devil shall have no residence in our children's lives, bodies and souls in Jesus Name. Father, we thank you for your Divine Healing Miracles in our children's lives.

We thank you, Lord, that our children shall live long lives and fulfil their purpose on earth in good health for your Divine Honour and Glory in Jesus Name.

AMEN

Is any among you afflicted? Let him pray.
Is any merry? Let him sing psalms.
Is any sick among you? Let him call for the elders of the church; and let them pray over him, anointing him with oil in the name of the Lord: And the prayer of faith shall save the sick, and the Lord shall raise him up; and if he have committed sins, they shall be forgiven him. Confess your faults one to another, and pray one for another, that ye may be healed. The effectual fervent prayer of a righteous man availeth much
James 5:13-16

Surely he hath borne our griefs, and carried our sorrows: yet we did esteem him stricken, smitten of God, and afflicted. But he was wounded for our transgressions, he was bruised for our iniquities: the chastisement of our peace was upon him; and with his stripes we are healed
Isaiah 53:4-5

For I will restore health unto thee, and I will heal thee of all thy wounds, saith the Lord; because they called thee and Outcast, saying, this is Zion, whom no man seeketh after
Jeremiah 30:17

5
PRAYER FOR SAFETY AND PROTECTION

Heavenly Father you are great and greatly to be praised. Father of Heaven and Earth we ask that you keep our children under your mighty wings.

Lord, we ask that our children shall never experience any untimely death, untimely injuries, untimely sickness, untimely accidents and untimely disasters in Jesus Name.

Lord, we ask that you cover our children with the blood of Jesus that no weapon formed or fashioned against them shall prosper.

They shall be under your mighty blanket in their going in and coming out. Every kidnapper, rapist, murderer, thief, bully no matter who the enemy may try to use, in form or fashion shall not locate our children in Jesus Name.

Lord let every weapon formed or fashioned to steal, kill and destroy our children be consumed to ashes now in Jesus Name. Lord fill our children with the spirit of discernment to discern their whereabouts and the people around them wherever they may go.

Lord let them hear your voice and obey it through the power of your Holy Spirit. Father, we ask that you take full control of our children's lives, mind, heart and soul.

Father quicken and order their steps to lead them into your Holy place of righteousness.

We speak your abundant life over our children that they shall not die but live long and healthy lives in Jesus Name.

Lord continue to set our children apart for your purpose and we ask that you use them for your Honour and Glory in Jesus Mighty Name.

Every spirit of darkness shall have no access to our children's lives from this day forth in Jesus Name.

Every high thing shall not be able to hinder our children's progress and success in this present time till eternity in Jesus Name.

We declare and decree every plan of the devil to steal their joy shall not prosper in Jesus Name.

We declare and decree every plan of the devil to kill their destiny shall not prosper in Jesus Name.

We declare and decree every plan of the devil to destroy their purpose shall not prosper in Jesus Name.

We declare and decree our children are overcomers through the blood of the Lamb and the Words of their testimony in Jesus mighty and precious Name.

We thank you, Lord, for every angel of Heaven assigned to them to protect them in all their ways in Jesus Name.

We thank you, Lord, for your Divine Word of Truth that you shall not leave them nor forsake them in Jesus Mighty and Precious Name
AMEN

Be strong and of good courage, fear not, nor be afraid
of them: for the LORD thy God, he is that doth go
with thee; he will not fail thee, nor forsake thee
Deuteronomy 31:6

Thou art my hiding place; thou shalt preserve me from trouble;
thou shalt compass me about with songs of deliverance. Selah
Psalm 32:7

God is our refuge and strength, a very present help in trouble
Psalm 46:1

The name of the Lord is a strong tower; the
righteous runneth into it, and is safe
Proverbs 18:10

6
DESTINY – FULFILLING THEIR PURPOSE

Father, we thank you for your many Divine Blessings over our children's lives. Lord we just say thank you for being their Heavenly Father, their provider, their guide, their rock, their fortress and their shield.

Father, we declare your mighty hedge over the plans and purpose you have for them Lord. The plans to protect them, to give them hope and to give them a future.

We know and trust that your plans are never failing and it is all for your Glory and Honour. Father may our children greatest desire is to fulfil their purpose here on earth.

Lord we ask that by the power of your Holy Spirit guide them to fully walk in their Divine Purpose with the Permanent Divine Favour of God upon their lives.

Father cause them have that hunger and thirst to be set apart from this world and let their minds and thoughts set for the things that are above. That whatever they do they do it unto the Lord and not unto man till Thy Kingdom Come.

Father let every demon and devil that is after their destiny be destroyed now by the fire of the Holy Ghost in Jesus Name.

Every monitoring spirit that is secretly monitoring our children's progress towards the mark of their High Calling in Jesus Christ is cast down exposed and crushed now by the finger of God in Jesus Name.

Lord, we cover our children's minds and their hearts from going astray. Father they shall continually be in a humble desire to fulfil and accomplish their purpose in Jesus Name.

Lord we cover their thoughts with the blood of Jesus that shall destroy thoughts of doubt, discouragement and despair from their lives and we ask that you bring their minds and heart to the Mind and Heart of Christ in Jesus Name.

Father let the Power of your Holy Spirit guide and comfort them in this path to fulfil their destiny. Lord take away from them the things that are not pleasing to you that are doors to demonic hindrances and stumbling blocks in Jesus Name.

Father, we declare and decree our children are overcomers of this world and the things of this world and they shall surely be the ones that will pass down to the generations yet to come testimonies of your Divine Goodness and Mercy towards them.

They shall rise into the perfect plans you have for them to walk in the plans to prosper them and to enjoy the plans you have for them for their future in Jesus Mighty Name.

Amen

And we know that in all things work together for good to them that love God, to them who are called according to his purpose
Romans 8:28

According to the eternal purpose which he purposed in Christ Jesus our Lord: In whom we have boldness and access with confidence by the faith of him
Ephesians 3:11-12

Brethren, I count not myself to have apprehended: but this one thing I do, forgetting those things which are behind, and reaching forth unto those things which are before. I press toward the mark for the prize of the high calling of God in Christ Jesus
Philippians 3:13-14

7
WALKING IN THE LOVE OF CHRIST

Heavenly Father Lord we thank you for our precious children. Father, we Glorify your Holy Mighty & Precious Name. Lord, we thank you for all that you have done and all that you will continue to do in our lives in Jesus Name.

Lord may we only raise our children to do the things that are pleasing unto you. Father, we ask that you fill our children hearts with the Agape Love of Christ. Lord empower them to walk in the fullness of Christ love and the ways of Christ.

Let them be kind, loving, caring and generous to all that they may come in contact with. Let their vessels be overflowing with compassion towards others that they will reveal your image and likeness of you that will cause them to attract others to seek you for that same Shekinah Glory.

We declare and decree spirit of hate, anger, depression, bitterness and rage shall not locate our children and take any residence in their lives in the Name of Jesus Christ of Nazareth.

Father empower our children with the strength to overcome temptation that the enemy may use to try them. Father empower their mind, heart, body and spirit to overcome fear, intimidation and limitation.

Let your love be increased in them daily that the enemy will not have an entrance to enter into their lives that will bring them to any link of darkness.

Father, we ask that you perfect our children in the way of the Lord to Love you Lord with all their minds, hearts and strength and to love their neighbours, others and those they come in contact with daily as themselves.

We thank you, Lord, that from this day forth our children shall walk, talk and live in the Agape Love of Christ that shall guide them to win souls for your Divine Kingdom in Jesus Christ Name.

Amen.

For this cause I bow my knees unto the Father of our Lord Jesus Christ, of whom the whole family in heaven and earth is named.
That he would grant you, according to his riches of his glory,
   ✓ *to be strengthen with might by his Spirit in the inner-man,*
     ✓ *that Christ may dwell in your hearts by faith,*
      ✓ *being grounded and rooted in love,*
  ✓ *may be able to comprehend with all saints what is the breadth, and length, and depth, and height*
and to know the love of Christ, which passeth knowledge,
    ✓ *That ye may be filled with all the fullness of God*
Ephesians 3:14-19

Beloved, let us love one another: for love is of God; and every one that loveth is born of God, and knoweth God.
He that loveth not knoweth not God; for God is love. In this was manifested the love of God toward us, because that God sent his only begotten Son into the world, that we might live through him. Herein is love, not that we loved God, but that he loved us, and sent his Son to be the propitiation for our sins. Beloved, if God so loved us, we ought also to love one another
1ˢᵗ John 4:7

And this is love that we walk after his commandments.
This is the commandment, that, as ye have heard from the beginning ye should walk in it
2ⁿᵈ John 1:6

8
DELIVERANCE & LIBERTY
TO OUR YOUTHS

Heavenly Father we love you, Lord. We love you today, tomorrow and forever Father.

Father we just want to say thank you for all your goodness and sweet mercy towards us Lord.

Father, we ask that you deliver our youths from every force of darkness that surrounds them. Father bring everything that is not of you in them to the feet of Jesus Christ.

Lord let your mighty power bring our youth's minds to the Mind of Christ in Jesus Name.

Everything that the enemy has ministered to our youths shall not take residence in their lives in Jesus Name.

Father by your mighty hand we destroy every stronghold the enemy has over our youth's lives that has kept them in bondage in Jesus Name.

Every manner of curse, hex, occult, voodoo, witchcraft, evil altars, demonic tents, evil dance and chats sent to destroy our youth's lives shall not prosper or prevail against them in Jesus Name.

We declare and decree every secret agent of the enemy deceiving our youth's lives shall be exposed and consumed to ashes in Jesus Name.

Our youths are free and shall be delivered from all forms of darkness physically, mentally, socially, academically and spiritually in Jesus Name.

We declare the backing of Heaven shall bring them into that place of Love, Joy, Peace, Unity and Liberty in Jesus Name.

Father by the finger of God we break all manner of generational curses of failure, discouragement, offensiveness, ignorance, idolatry, stagnation and pride from off our youth's lives that may have taken any roots in their hearts with the mighty undefeated blood of Jesus.

Lord, we declare your Divine Promised Word over our youth's lives that who the son has set free is free indeed.

Therefore, we declare and decree our youths are free and delivered right now to do great and mighty things for your Kingdom in Jesus Name.

We declare and decree our youths shall operate in the Divine Wisdom of God and they shall overcome all the foolish things of this world and the world yet to come in Jesus Name.

They shall run and not grow weary. They shall be filled with the fire of the Holy Ghost to war against the principalities and the forces of darkness seen and unseen in Jesus Name.

They shall be vessels of Honour and Holiness from this day forth representing and revealing the image and likeness of your Divine character as a light on this earth in Jesus Name.

Amen

And it shall come to pass in the last days, saith God,
> ✓ *I will pour out of my Spirit upon all flesh:*
> ✓ *And your sons and your daughters shall prophesy,*
> ✓ *And your young men shall see visions,*
> ✓ *And your old men shall dream dreams:*
> ✓ *And on my servants*
> ✓ *and on my handmaidens I will pour out in those days of my Spirit; and they shall prophesy*
Acts 2: 17-21

> ✓ *Let no one [despise your youth,*
> ✓ *but be an example to the believers in word,*
> ✓ *in conduct,*
> ✓ *in love,*

✓ *in spirit,*
✓ *in faith,*
✓ *in purity.*

Till I come,

✓ *Give attention to reading,*
✓ *to exhortation,*
✓ *to doctrine.*

✓ *Do not neglect the gift that is in you, which was given to you by prophecy with the laying on of the hands of the eldership.*
✓ *Meditate on these things; give yourself entirely to them, that your progress may be evident to all.*

✓ *Take heed to yourself and to the doctrine.*

✓ *Continue in them, for in doing this you will save both yourself and those who hear you.*
Timothy 4:12-16

9
DISMANTLING THE PLANS OF THE ENEMY FROM OUR CHILDREN'S LIVES

Our children shall live and not die in Jesus Name.

Our children shall walk, talk and affiliate in Godly counsel aware and unaware at all times in Jesus Name.

Our children shall be overcomers through the blood of the Lamb and the Words of their Testimonies in Jesus Name.

Our children shall triumphant over every plan and deceitful scheme of the enemy in Jesus Name.

Our children shall be the head and not the tail, they shall be above and not beneath in Jesus Name.

The devil shall have no foothold, spell hold, pledge hold or any form of strong hold in our children's lives in Jesus Name.

Every evil agent of Satan sent to mislead our children into the spell of darkness shall be terminated by fire and consumed to ashes in Jesus Name.

Every evil agenda the enemy has against our children's destiny is terminated now by fire in Jesus Name.

We declare and decree no untimely death, untimely sickness, untimely accident, untimely injury and untimely disaster shall locate our children in Jesus Name.

Every tent practising witchcraft and voodoo against our children shall be dismantled now in Jesus Name.

Any witchcraft sent to frustrate our children to misery and confusion shall be consumed to ashes now by Fire in Jesus Name.

Every spirit of idleness, laziness and stagnation in our children's lives be uprooted now in Jesus Name.

Every spirit of discouragement sent to destroy our children's progress and growth physically, mentally, naturally, academically, financially and spiritually shall fall and die now in the mighty Name of Jesus.

Amen

10
SPEAKING DIVINE BLESSINGS INTO OUR CHILDREN'S LIVES

Our children shall live, breathe, see, hear and Walk in the fullness of God all the days of their lives In Jesus Name.

The Lord of Heaven shall bless our children, cause His Face to shine on them. He shall keep and prosper them all the days of their lives in Jesus Name.

The Lord shall increase in our children Divine Wisdom, Knowledge, Understanding, Stature and Favour with God and man in Jesus Name.

Our children shall rise and worship the Lord in Spirit and Truth in Jesus Name.

Our children shall be grounded and rooted in Christ Jesus all the days of their lives.

Our children shall be used by God as Samuel and David in their tender age In Jesus Name.

Our children shall be filled with the Overflowing Agape Love of Christ to love and forgive others as the Lord loves and forgive us in Jesus Name.

Our children shall do great and mighty things for the Glory of God.

Our children shall live, eat and drink from the overflowing fountain of God in Jesus Name.

We declare and decree the utterance of Praise and Thanksgiving shall be on our children's lips all the days of their lives in Jesus Name.

We declare and decree our children are blessed and highly favoured by God.

We declare and decree our children are supernaturally blessed and shall be successful in everything they set their hearts to do physically, mentally, academically, financially and spiritually in Jesus Mighty Name.

Amen

Matthew 18:6 KJV
But whoso shall offend one of
these little ones which believe in
me, it were better for him that a
millstone were hanged about his
neck, and that he were drowned
in the depth of the sea.

11
DEDICATION

I am honoured to dedicate this book "Praying for Our Precious Children, Volume 1" to my four (4) wonderful children Satesh, Ranjeev, Adrion and Emily.

I love you all very much and I thank God for giving me each of you. All four (4) of you complete me. I am not where I am and who I am without you. You are part of my purpose and my destiny and I am honoured to be part of yours and to be called your mom.

I pray that the Lord do great and mighty things through you for His glory and honour.

You were born to be leaders and so shall May the Lord continue to bless each of you from Glory to Glory and Strength to Strength in Jesus Name.

Amen

The LORD bless thee
Keep thee:
The LORD make his face shine upon thee,
And be gracious unto thee:
The LORD lift up his countenance upon thee,
And give thee peace
Numbers 6:24-26

12
A NOTE TO THE PRAYER WARRIOR

Thank you, beloved Prayer Warrior, chosen by God, to intercede for our precious children.

Whether you are a parent or not, you are fulfilling your duty to bring up our children in the way that they should go so that when they get old enough they surely will not depart from it.

The Lord has used many men and women in the bible to prayer especially prayer for others. He used Moses to bring His Children out of Egypt (darkness) and furnished them with many miracles, signs and wonders and this is exactly what God is using us to do and it all starts with Prayer and Praying for others.

I declare that all that you have asked for our Precious Children of this Universe will come to pass according to the perfect will of God.

I declare that all these prayers are going to manifest in your child's/ children's lives as you speak it over them with the backing of Heaven to perform all things in Jesus Name.

Amen

I thank my God always on your behalf, for the grace
of God which is given you by Jesus Christ;
That in everything ye are enriched by him, in all utterance, and in
all knowledge; Even as the testimony of Christ was confirmed in you:
So that ye come behind in no gift; waiting for
the coming of our Lord Jesus Christ:

*Who shall also confirm you unto the end, that ye may
be blameless in the day of our Lord Jesus Christ
1ˢᵗ Corinthians 1:7*

If you have any comments or inquiries, please feel free to contact me and would love to hear of your supernatural breakthroughs and testimonies. Any special prayer request please let me know, I will make myself available to go before our Heavenly Father for you and your loved ones. God's Blessings to you Beloved Prayer Warrior. Continue to Prayer for Our Precious Children. I love you!

*I will praise thee; for I am fearfully and wonderfully made:
marvellous are thy works; and that my soul knoweth right well
Psalms 139:14*

THE END

Author: SHARMELA GOKOOL
Country: *Trinidad, West Indies*
Email: *sharmela_gokool@hotmail.com*
Facebook Page:
Praying For Our Precious Children
https://www.facebook.com/groups/praying4ourpreciouschildren/

Coming Soon:
Praying for Our Precious Children
Volume Two (2)
"Declaring the word and activating its Power"

Printed in the United States
By Bookmasters